D1373705

5/10

Baby Cats

Bobbie Kalman

🌳 Crabtree Publishing Company

www.crabtreebooks.com

It's fun to learn about Baby Animals

Created by Bobbie Kalman

For baby Dexter Peter Crabtree, our new grandson.
We welcome you to the world with all our love.
Grandma Bobbie and Grandpa Peter

**Author and
Editor-in-Chief**
Bobbie Kalman

Editor
Robin Johnson

Photo research
Crystal Sikkens

Design
Katherine Kantor
Samantha Crabtree (cover)

Production coordinator
Katherine Kantor

Illustrations
Bonna Rouse: pages 22, 24

Photographs
© iStockphoto.com: pages 9 (bottom), 14 (bottom left),
     15 (top left), 24 (bottom right)
© 2008 Jupiterimages Corporation: pages 1 (middle), 7
© Shutterstock.com: cover, pages 1 (all except middle),
     4, 6, 8, 9 (top), 10, 11 (bottom), 12, 13, 14 (top right),
     15 (middle and bottom), 17 (top), 18 (top), 20,
     21 (all except top left), 23, 24 (all except bottom right)
Other images by Corel, Creatas, Digital Vision,
     and Photodisc

Library and Archives Canada Cataloguing in Publication

Kalman, Bobbie, 1947-
    Baby cats / Bobbie Kalman.

(It's fun to learn about baby animals)
Includes index.
ISBN 978-0-7787-3951-7 (bound).--ISBN 978-0-7787-3970-8 (pbk.)

    1. Felidae--Infancy--Juvenile literature. 2. Kittens--Juvenile
literature.
I. Title. II. Series.

QL737.C23K33 2008   j599.75'139   C2008-900142-7

Library of Congress Cataloging-in-Publication Data

Kalman, Bobbie.
    Baby cats / Bobbie Kalman.
        p. cm. -- (It's fun to learn about baby animals)
    Includes index.
    ISBN-13: 978-0-7787-3951-7 (rlb)
    ISBN-10: 0-7787-3951-1 (rlb)
    ISBN-13: 978-0-7787-3970-8 (pb)
    ISBN-10: 0-7787-3970-8 (pb)
    1. Felidae--Infancy--Juvenile literature. 2. Kittens--Juvenile literature.
I. Title.
    QL737.C23K33 2008
    599.75'5139--dc22
                                    2008005387

Crabtree Publishing Company

www.crabtreebooks.com   1-800-387-7650

Published in Canada
Crabtree Publishing
616 Welland Ave.
St. Catharines, Ontario
L2M 5V6

Published in the United States
Crabtree Publishing
PMB16A
350 Fifth Ave., Suite 3308
New York, NY 10118

Published in the United Kingdom
Crabtree Publishing
White Cross Mills
High Town, Lancaster
LA1 4XS

Published in Australia
Crabtree Publishing
386 Mt. Alexander Rd.
Ascot Vale (Melbourne)
VIC 3032

What is in this book?

What is a cat?

Cats are animals called **mammals**. You are a mammal, too. Mammals are born. Mammals have hair or fur. Cats have fur.

This cat was just born. Baby cats cannot see when they are born.

This baby cat will not see well until it is about ten weeks old.

Mother cats have **litters** of babies. A litter is more than two babies. Mammal mothers feed their babies milk. The milk is made inside the bodies of the mothers. These baby tigers are drinking their mother's milk.

Cats, cats, cats

Meow!

Meow!

Meow!

There are many kinds of cats. Some cats are **pet cats**. Pet cats live with people. Baby pet cats are called **kittens**. Do you have a kitten?

Meow!

Meow!

Some cats do not live with people.
They are **wild cats**. Wild cats live
outdoors in nature. Baby wild cats are
called **cubs**. This lynx cub is a wild cat.

A cat's body

A cat has four legs. A cat has a tail. Fur covers a cat's body. A cat has bones inside its body.

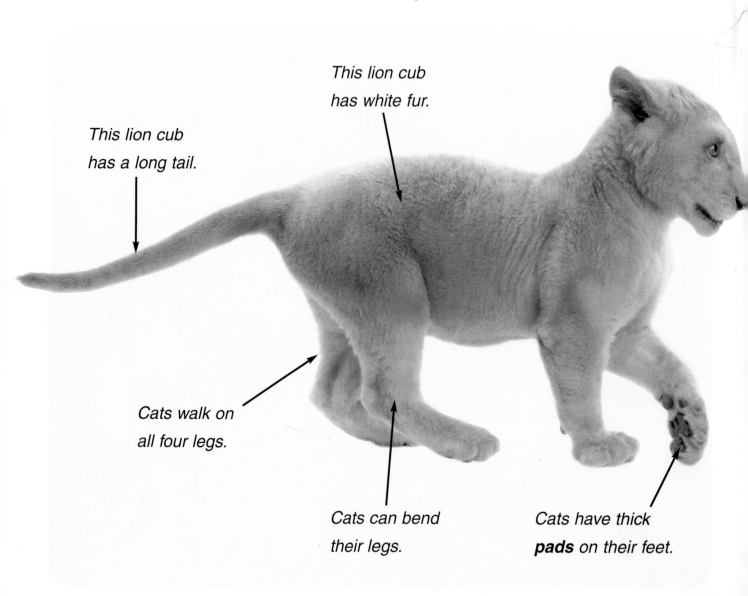

This lion cub has white fur.

This lion cub has a long tail.

Cats walk on all four legs.

Cats can bend their legs.

Cats have thick **pads** on their feet.

Cats have **claws** on their feet. Claws are curved nails.

Cats have **backbones**. Backbones are the bones in the middle of an animal's back. Animals with backbones are called **vertebrates**. Cats are vertebrates. You are a vertebrate, too.

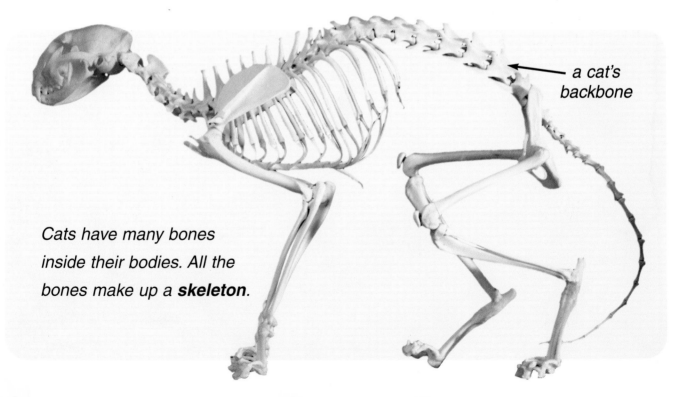

a cat's backbone

Cats have many bones inside their bodies. All the bones make up a **skeleton**.

Cat coats

Some baby cats have fur that is one color. This kitten is black. The lion cub is white. It looks like a little lamb!

lion cub

tiger cub

lynx cub

Many baby cats have **patterns** on their fur. Spots and stripes are patterns. Which pattern does the tiger cub have on its coat? Which pattern does the lynx cub have on its coat?

Cat senses

You have five **senses**. They are sight, hearing, smell, touch, and taste. Cats also have senses. Senses help cats learn about their world. Cats need their senses to stay alive.

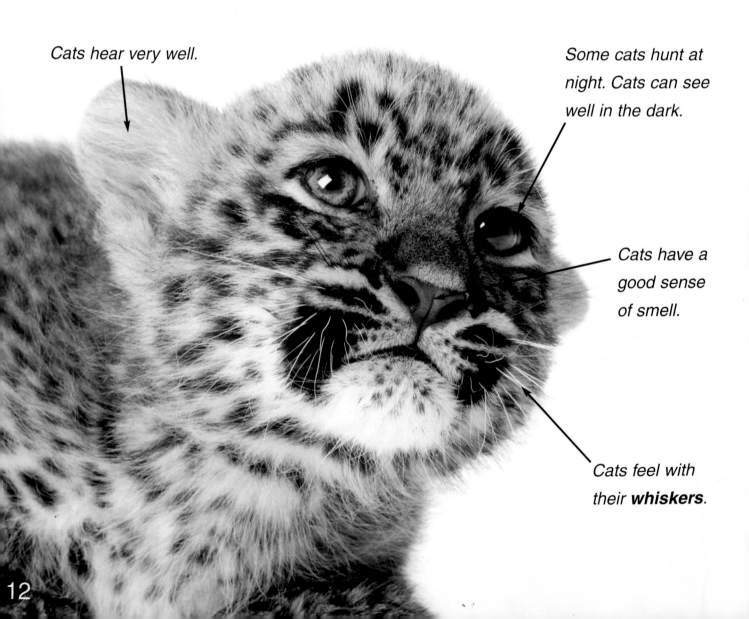

Cats hear very well.

Some cats hunt at night. Cats can see well in the dark.

Cats have a good sense of smell.

Cats feel with their **whiskers**.

Cats taste with their tongues. They smell with their noses. Cats also smell with the **roofs**, or tops, of their mouths. Their mouths can smell other animals.

A cat has sharp teeth and a bumpy tongue.

Big cats, little cats

Cats are not all the same size. There are big cats, and there are little cats. Tigers are the biggest cats. Some big cats **roar**. A roar is a very loud sound. This tiger cub will roar when it grows up.

tiger cub

This lion cub will grow to be as big as its mother. It will also roar.

Leopards are big cats, too. Leopards make loud growling sounds.

cheetahs

Cheetahs are smaller than tigers and lions. They are the fastest runners of all the cats.

Lynxes are medium-sized cats. They are smaller than cheetahs.

Pet cats are little cats. Little cats meow. What sound do pet cats make when they are happy?

Purrrr Purrrr

Where do cats live?

The natural places where animals live are called **habitats**. Wild cats live in different kinds of habitats. This lynx cub lives in a **forest** habitat. Forests are habitats with many trees.

lynx cub

This lynx cub lives inside a tree log in a forest.

lion cub

cougar cub

This lion cub lives in a hot **grassland** habitat. Grasslands are flat habitats where grasses, bushes, and a few trees grow. This cougar cub lives on a mountain. Its habitat is cold and snowy in winter.

Cat families

Most wild cat families are made up of mothers and their cubs. The mothers feed the cubs. After a few months, they teach the cubs how to find their own food. Cubs stay with their mothers for up to two years.

mane

female

female cub

male

*Lion families are bigger than most cat families are. Lion families are called **prides**.*
*A lion pride is made up of a male, and some females, and cubs. A male lion has a **mane**.*

Mother cats keep their cubs safe. This mother bobcat is keeping her cub from falling off a rock.

Many mother cats hide their cubs. They move them when the cubs are in danger. This mother cougar is carrying her cub by the **scruff** of its neck. Carrying a cub this way does not hurt the cub. It keeps the cub calm.

Learning to hunt

Cats are **carnivores**. Carnivores eat mainly meat. Cats are also **predators**. Predators hunt the animals they eat. Cubs learn how to hunt by playing.

*Cats run and chase their **prey**. Prey are the animals they hunt. These cougar cubs are racing each other. When they are adults, they will need to run very fast to catch prey.*

lynx cub

cheetah cub

tiger cub

Cubs must climb trees if they want to hunt birds.

They have to keep their eyes open to spot prey.

Stalking means sneaking quietly after prey.

lion cubs

When cats **pounce**, they jump on top of prey. This cub is practicing on its sister.

Play hunting is hard work! This lion cub is very tired. It is time to take a nap!

Growing and changing

Cats go through a set of changes called a **life cycle**. A life cycle starts when a cub or kitten is born. The young cat grows and changes. Over time, it becomes an adult cat. These pictures show the life cycle of a lion.

A baby lion drinks its mother's milk.

A young lion grows bigger and stronger.

Adult lions can make babies.

Male lion cubs leave the pride after two years. They sometimes live together for a while. Then they find prides of their own and start new families.

A new life cycle starts with every baby that is born.

Words to Know and Index

bodies
pages 5, 8-9

cubs
pages 7, 8, 10, 11, 14, 16, 17, 18, 19, 20, 21, 22, 23

families
pages 18-19, 23

fur
pages 4, 8, 10-11

habitats
pages 16-17

hunting
pages 12, 20-21

kittens
pages 6, 10, 22

life cycle
pages 22-23

mammals
pages 4-5

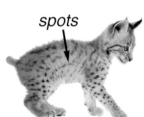

spots

patterns
page 11

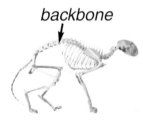

backbone

vertebrates
page 9

Other index words
carnivores page 20
litters page 5
predators page 20
prey pages 20, 21
senses pages 12-13